HiPPOBOTTOMUS

Didier Lévy and Marc Boutavant

HIPPOBOTTOMUS

t&h

It’s that time of day when all the animals go down to the river bank for a drink of water.

Everybody’s happy, but not the hippopotamus.

'You look worried. What's wrong?'
the elephant asks.

'My bottom's too big,'
says the hippopotamus.

'Can we have a look at it?' the other animals ask.

Slowly, the hippo turns around.

The animals have a good look at the hippo's bottom.

Some compare it to their own bottom. Some try to measure it. Some just stare at it and don't say a word.

Other animals see the crowd and stop to find out what's going on. Soon, the whole forest is talking about the hippo's bottom.

But nobody can agree.

The ones who have big bottoms say 'Isn't it small!'

The ones who have small bottoms say 'Isn't it big!'

And between those two opinions, there are other animals who think it's fairly large or slightly small or pretty average.

The size of the hippo's bottom becomes the number one topic of conversation.

Each side tries its best to beat the others. Things get louder and louder. The talking turns into an argument. And some of the words get rather rude!

Then one group of animals (it's hard to tell which one) starts to throw rotten fruit at the others.

Pretty soon, the air is full of flying objects!

The hippopotamus watches in shock as the fur flies.

'Calm down, everybody!' he yells. 'Please stop fighting!'

But it's no use. Nobody's listening.

So the hippopotamus shrugs and walks away.
Suddenly he feels a need to do something...

…and the need is getting stronger! He starts to run…

...until he finds his potty and sits down. Ahhhh.
What a relief. Peace and quiet at last!

The hippopotamus sighs. 'I was worried for no reason,' he thinks. 'My bottom is just the right size!'

Suddenly the elephant feels a sudden need
to leave the fight and find her own potty.

So do the chimp, the crocodile, the vulture and the zebra.

Soon all the animals are sitting on their potties. Ahhhh.

Pretty soon, they're all smiling and chatting. They don't even remember what they were fighting about.

The hippo finishes first. He gets up and picks a clean leaf for each animal, as a way to say sorry for all the trouble.

Because a nice soft leaf is the best way to wipe your bottom, no matter what size it is.

Translated from the French *Le popotin de l'hippopo* by Jill Phythian

First published in the United Kingdom in 2024
by Thames & Hudson Ltd, 181A High Holborn,
London WC1V 7QX

British Library Cataloguing-in-Publication Data
A catalogue record for this book is available from the British Library

ISBN 978-0-500-65361-6

Printed and bound in China by C&C Offset Printing Co. Ltd.

FSC www.fsc.org
MIX
Paper | Supporting responsible forestry
FSC® C008047